OUR
CHANGING
EARTH

CLIMATE CHANGE

Jason D. Nemeth

PowerKiDS
press.
New York

Published in 2012 by The Rosen Publishing Group, Inc.
29 East 21st Street, New York, NY 10010

First Edition

Editor: Amelie von Zumbusch
Book Design: Greg Tucker

Photo Credits: Cover, pp. 4, 5, 6, 7, 9, 10, 11, 12, 15 (right), 16–17, 18–19, 19 (top) 22 Shutterstock.com; p. 8 George F. Mobley/National Geographic/Getty Images; p. 13 Goodshoot/Thinkstock; p. 14 Comstock/Thinkstock; p. 15 (left) Ian McKinnell/Getty Images; p. 20 Phil Walter/Getty Images; p. 21 Mike Theiss/National Geographic/Getty Images.

Library of Congress Cataloging-in-Publication Data

Nemeth, Jason D.
 Climate change / by Jason D. Nemeth. — 1st ed.
     p. cm. — (Our changing earth)
 Includes index.
 ISBN 978-1-4488-6166-8 (library binding) — ISBN 978-1-4488-6290-0 (pbk.) — ISBN 978-1-4488-6291-7 (6-pack)
 1. Climatic changes—Juvenile literature. 2. Global warming—Juvenile literature. I. Title.
 QC981.8.C5N428 2012
 551.6—dc23
                          2011021287

Manufactured in the United States of America

CPSIA Compliance Information: Batch #WW12PK: For Further Information contact Rosen Publishing, New York, New York at 1-800-237-9932

CONTENTS

WEATHER AND CLIMATE

Would you like to take a vacation to the rain forests of Antarctica? To do this, you would need to travel back in time. Today, Antarctica is cold and snow covered. It had a hot, rainy **climate** 250 million years ago, though. Climate is the pattern of weather in a place. There is a difference between climate and

The Sahara is now a sandy desert. It had a different climate between 10,000 and 8,000 years ago, though. It was a grassland with lots of plants and animals.

weather. Weather is what happens today, this month, or this year. Climate is the normal weather over a long time.

Over Earth's history, its climates have gone through many changes. They continue to change today. In fact, scientists have learned that people are making climate change happen faster than it would naturally.

Scientists have found that the glaciers, or ice sheets, on Oregon's Mount Hood are melting. This is an example of a climate change that is happening today.

Evergreen forests called taiga are found in northern lands with very cold, snowy winters and warm, wet summers. These places have almost no spring or fall.

What would you expect a desert to be like? If you said dry, you would be right. Deserts get very little rainfall. This gives them dry climates. Climates are defined by their average **temperatures** and amounts of **precipitation**. Temperature is a measure of how hot or cold something is. Precipitation is rain or snow.

Different places have different climates. The Sahara is a sandy desert in Africa. It has a hot, dry climate. South America's Amazon rain forest is hot and gets lots of rain all year long. **Chaparral** is found in parts of California. Its climate has hot, dry summers and cool, wet winters.

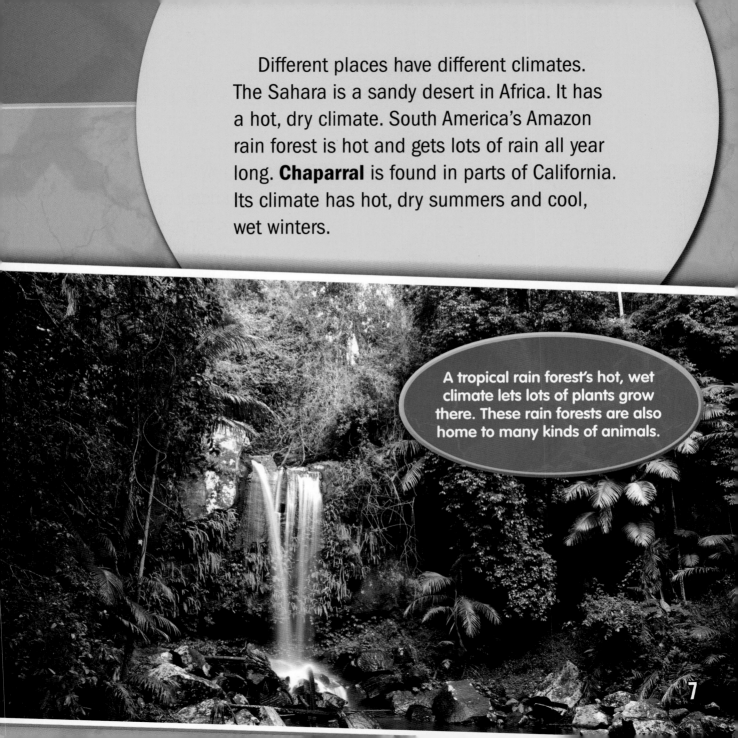

A tropical rain forest's hot, wet climate lets lots of plants grow there. These rain forests are also home to many kinds of animals.

CLIMATE CLUES

Scientists know that Earth's climate has changed over time because these changes left their traces on Earth. Scientists drill deep into **glaciers** to pull out pieces of ice. Glaciers are big sheets of ice that built up over time. Tiny air bubbles got trapped inside glacier ice as it formed. They tell scientists what the climate was like when they got trapped.

This scientist is taking samples of ice in Kluane National Park, in Canada. He plans to study the amount of a gas called carbon dioxide in the ice.

Scientists also look at tree rings for clues about what the climate was like in the past. Many kinds of trees add one new ring to their trunks each year. Wider rings form during years in which spring is warmer than usual.

This is the fossil, or remains, of a fish that lived long ago. The fossil helps us figure out that the land where it was found must once have been covered by water.

CLIMATE'S BIG BANGS

Erupting **volcanoes** can cause climate change. They shoot ash and gas high into the **atmosphere**, or layer of gases around Earth. Energy from the Sun passes through the atmosphere and warms Earth. When volcanoes erupt, some of the ash and gas from them stays in the atmosphere. This blocks part of the Sun's energy. On Earth, temperatures fall. In 1991, Mt. Pinatubo erupted in

Volcanoes are openings in Earth's outside. From time to time, they erupt. In an eruption, ash, gas, rocks, or melted rock, called lava, flows out of a volcano.

the Philippines. It lowered temperatures on Earth for the next two years.

When a **meteorite**, or object from space, crashes into Earth, it also sends lots of dust into the atmosphere. This causes climate change, too. Many scientists believe that this is what killed the dinosaurs.

A meteorite that hit Earth about 50,000 years ago formed Arizona's Meteor Crater. The crash sent rock flying and left a crater about 4,000 feet (1,219 m) wide.

WARMING UP AND COOLING OFF

Most of Earth's warmth comes from the Sun. However, the Sun sometimes cools down a bit and produces less energy. When this happens, Earth gets less energy and cools, too. In the seventeenth century, a cool Sun helped cause a cool period on Earth. This time was known as the **Little Ice Age**.

The Gulf Stream is a current in the Atlantic Ocean. It brings warm water up the coast of North America and toward Europe. It warms the climate of places such as Scotland's Isle of Lewis.

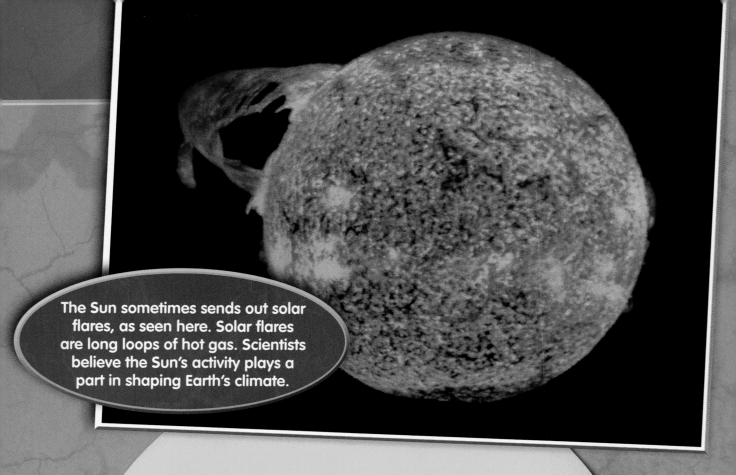

The Sun sometimes sends out solar flares, as seen here. Solar flares are long loops of hot gas. Scientists believe the Sun's activity plays a part in shaping Earth's climate.

Earth's oceans also have an effect on climate. Their water soaks up some of the Sun's energy. This keeps Earth cool.

Ocean **currents** move warm or cold water throughout Earth's oceans. The water warms or cools nearby land, too. If the flow of ocean currents changes, that can cause climate change, too.

EARTH'S BLANKET

Earth's atmosphere is made up of water vapor and other gases. The mix of gases has changed over time. Some of these gases came out of Earth when volcanoes erupted. Living things produce other gases. For example, plants and tiny living things called algae make the gas **oxygen**.

Gases in the atmosphere do different jobs. Some, such

People and other animals breathe in oxygen. We need oxygen to stay alive.

as **ozone**, keep harmful rays from the Sun out. Others, such as **carbon dioxide**, keep the Sun's heat in. Gases that keep the Sun's heat in are called greenhouse gases. Without them, Earth would be too cold for life to grow and survive.

TOP: Plants need sunlight, water, and carbon dioxide to make oxygen. **LEFT:** Earth's atmosphere keeps it from getting too hot or too cold. Mercury has no atmosphere. The difference in temperature between night and day there is about 1,058° F (653° C).

The presence of too many greenhouse gases in the atmosphere causes global warming. Global warming means that Earth is getting hotter. It happens because the extra greenhouse gases trap more of the Sun's heat. Sometimes this happens naturally. Today, though, it is happening faster than it should.

The extra greenhouse gases are coming from people. Fuels like coal and oil trap these gases. When we burn coal and oil for energy, the gases are released. We use this energy to run our cars, planes, and trains. We also use it to heat our homes and schools. However, it is heating up the whole Earth as well.

Global warming is melting Earth's glaciers. Briksdalsbreen is a glacier in Norway. Between 2001 and 2006, it melted so much that it became about 984 feet (300 m) shorter.

EARTH OUT OF BALANCE

Balance is important to Earth's climate. Some things create greenhouse gases and other things trap them. People release carbon dioxide when we breathe. However, trees and other plants use that carbon dioxide to make food and grow.

The Aral Sea once covered the land where this boat sits. In the 1960s, people started taking water from it to grow crops. Today, most of its water has dried up.

People cut down forests for many reasons. Some trees are used to make paper. Trees also supply wood that is used to build houses, tables, and chairs.

We upset that balance when we change the world too quickly. When we cut down forests, we leave fewer trees to take in carbon dioxide. More carbon dioxide gets into the atmosphere.

When farm animals eat the plants in grasslands, it also causes problems. Plants hold soil in place. Without them, wind blows the soil away. The land turns into a desert where few plants grow.

TRACKING CLIMATE CHANGE

Scientists use many methods to track the climate change that is happening today. They record daily temperatures and rainfall all over the world. Some scientists also measure gases in the atmosphere, ocean temperatures, and weather patterns. Some even study bird **migration** patterns. In 2005, scientists found that the places where many North American birds spent the winter tended not to be as far south as they had been 40 years before.

This scientist is studying Australia's Daintree Rainforest. She wants to see if global warming is causing problems for the plants and animals that live there.

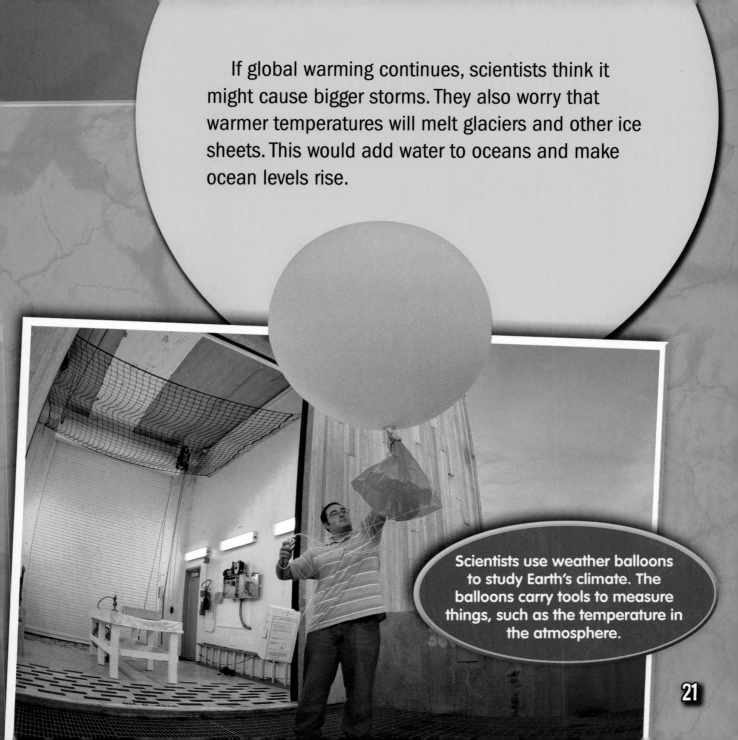

If global warming continues, scientists think it might cause bigger storms. They also worry that warmer temperatures will melt glaciers and other ice sheets. This would add water to oceans and make ocean levels rise.

Scientists use weather balloons to study Earth's climate. The balloons carry tools to measure things, such as the temperature in the atmosphere.

Tomorrow's climate depends on the choices we make today. Burning fossil fuels is a major source of greenhouse gases. Switching to clean energy, such as solar power and wind power, can help slow climate change. Using less energy helps, too.

Replanting trees will soak up some of the carbon dioxide we make. In some places, people are also returning wetlands and grasslands to their natural state. These are just some of the actions we can take today to bring Earth's climate back into balance.

Riding your bike produces less greenhouse gases than riding in a car.

GLOSSARY

atmosphere (AT-muh-sfeer) The gases around an object in space. On Earth this is air.

carbon dioxide (KAHR-bun dy-OK-syd) A gas with no smell or color. People breathe out carbon dioxide.

chaparral (sha-puh-RAL) An environment with woody plants and with dry summers and wet winters.

climate (KLY-mut) The kind of weather a certain place has.

currents (KUR-ents) Water that flows in one direction.

glaciers (GLAY-shurz) Large masses of ice that move down mountains or along valleys.

Little Ice Age (LIH-tel YS AYJ) A period in the seventeenth century when Earth cooled a little bit.

meteorite (MEE-tee-uh-ryt) A rock from outer space that reaches Earth's surface.

migration (my-GRAY-shun) The movement of people or animals from one place to another.

oxygen (OK-sih-jen) A gas that has no color or taste and is necessary for people and animals to breathe.

ozone (OH-zohn) A gas that forms from oxygen.

precipitation (preh-sih-pih-TAY-shun) Any moisture that falls from the sky. Rain and snow are precipitation.

temperatures (TEM-pur-cherz) Measures of how hot or cold things are.

volcanoes (vol-KAY-nohz) Openings that sometimes shoots up hot, melted rock called lava.

INDEX

WEB SITES

Due to the changing nature of Internet links, PowerKids Press has developed an
online list of Web sites related to the subject of this book. This site is updated regularly.
Please use this link to access the list:
www.powerkidslinks.com/chng/climate/